THE PENULTIMATE DATING GUIDE FOR MEN

A DON J. ADAMS WRITE YOUR ADVENTURE SERIES BOOK

EDITED & ILLUSTRATED BY YOU!

NEVER PROPOSE

ON

A FIRST OR

SECOND

DATE.

92% OF WOMEN AGREE, THEY ALL HAVE DREAMT OF A PROPOSAL AT A STADIUM ON THE JUMBOTRON SINCE THEY WERE LITTLE GIRLS.

MAKE

SURE

TO

WAIT UNTIL AT LEAST

THE THIRD DATE   FOR

THE STADIUM PROPOSAL.

IF YOU

HAVE AN ITEM

ENDING ON EBAY

OR ARE UNDER ATTACK ON

AN

APP

ITS OKAY TO CHECK

EVERY FEW MINUTES ON

YOUR DATE.   SHE LL

UNDERSTAND.

BEFORE SHE ARRIVES AT THE RESTAURANT ORDER FOR HER. SHE'LL JUST ORDER THE SALAD ANYWAY.

IT'S OKAY TO SHOW UP
IN   REGULAR JEANS AND
AN UNDERSHIRT.

WHY COMB YOUR HAIR?
YOU'RE NOT   AT
WORK.

—BESIDES SHE'S
SUPPOSED TO BE
THE ONE   THAT
LOOKS GOOD FOR YOU.

ONLY FOCUS ON HER. DON T LET OTHERS RUIN YOUR DATE. TELL THAT MOTHER TO SHUT HER KIDS UP. WHY WOULD SHE BRING THEM TO THE RESTAURANT ANYWAY?

RESEARCH HAS SHOWN,
WOMEN ARE MOST
ATTRACTED   TO
THEIR PERFECT
MATE S   SCENT.
DON T   SHOWER FOR
A FEW DAYS BEFORE YOUR
FIRST DATE.   IT WILL
INCREASE YOUR   ODDS.

NEVER WEAR COLOGNE OR AFTERSHAVE. IT ALSO RUINS THAT NATURAL SCENT ALL WOMEN CRAVE. IT DRIVES THEM WILD.

DATING GURUS AND BROS ALL TELL YOU TO BE SMOOTH. DON'T FORGET TO SHAVE EVERYTHING. WOMEN LIKE A SMOOTH MAN.

OUT TO A MOVIE?

LUNCH?

MINI GOLF?

IF   AN EMPLOYEE
     ASKS HER   WHAT SHE
     WANTS

REMEMBER, YOU   SET
UP THE DATE   NOT
HER.   ALWAYS
ANSWER FOR HER.

OUT FOR DINNER? MAKE SURE TO LET HER KNOW IF SHE EATS TOO FAST, OR SLOW, OR TOO LOUD, OR TOO MUCH. WOMEN LOVE TALKING ABOUT FOOD AND HOW YOU NOTICE THEM EATING IT.

NERVOUS ABOUT YOUR DATE?

DRINK A FEW BEERS AND

SLAM SOME SHOTS. ALCOHOL WILL LOOSEN YOU UP.

HOW DID YOUR LAST RELATIONSHIP END?

SHE'LL WANT TO KNOW. MAKE SURE TO PREPARE. IF FOR SOME REASON SHE FORGETS TO ASK, TELL HER EVERY DETAIL.

PRO TIP: CALL HER BY YOUR MOMS NAME. WHEN SHE CORRECTS YOU, TELL HER SORRY AND THAT SHE REMINDS YOU OF YOUR MOTHER.

SUPER PRO TIP: IF YOU KNOW HER MOTHER, CALL HER BY HER MOTHERS NAME. APOLOGIZE AND TELL HER HOW MUCH SHE REMINDS YOU OF HER MOTHER.

IT'S GOOD TO GET THINGS OUT IN THE OPEN.   MAKE SURE TO TALK ABOUT WHO YOU VOTE OR WOULD NOT VOTE FOR   AND WHY.   ALL NEWS TOPICS ARE FAIR GAME.   NOBODY LIKES TO TALK ABOUT THE WEATHER.

ASK HER HOW MANY

CHILDREN SHE WANTS.

IMMEDIATELY AGREE.

MAKE SURE TO PAY THE ENTIRE BILL.

DON T LET HER SPLIT.

WHO S THE MAN?

YOU ARE.

WOMEN NEVER ARE
THEMSELVES ON A DATE.
-SO ITS OKAY   TO
PRETEND TO BE SOMEONE
YOU ARE NOT.

ITS IMPORTANT TO REMEMBER WOMEN DON T GET NERVOUS. ITS JUST YOU. IF SHE DOES SOMETHING OUT IF THE ORDINARY, MAKE SURE TO POINT IT OUT .

ALSO - MAKE SURE SHE APOLOGIZES.

IF SHE HAS TO USE THE LADIES ROOM - THE DATE

MUST NOT BE GOING WELL. ITS OKAY TO SCOUT AND GRAB SOME DIGITS WHILE SHE - FRESHENS UP. -

BEST PLACES TO BREAK UP

IF YOU ARE STRUGGLING TO MOVE FORWARD ON YOUR DATE. TEXT YOUR EX, SHE WILL KNOW WHAT TO DO.

STICKING OUT WILL GET WOMEN TALKING ABOUT YOU AFTER YOUR DATE. SURPRISE HER - WEAR A ROMPER.

STUDY UP ON WOMEN S TOPICS BEFORE YOUR DATE - CLOTHES, SHOPPING, COOKING, CHOCOLATE, WINE-

DON T TALK ABOUT MANLY STUFF LIKE SPORTS OR WORK LIFE.

ALWAYS FOLLOW THESE FOUR STEPS WHEN CONFIRMING A DATE.

1. EMAIL HER THE WEEK BEFORE THE DATE.

2. TEXT HER THE NIGHT BEFORE.

3. TEXT HER. TELL HER SHES LATE.

4. MAIL HER A THANK YOU CARD.

WOMEN LOVE TREASURE HUNTS. LEAVE A NOTE LIKE- I SEE YOU. OR I KNOW WHERE YOU JOG.- ON THE TABLE BEFORE YOUR DATE ARRIVES. SIT A FEW TABLES AWAY, UNTIL SHE READS THE NOTE.

WORKS EVERY TIME.

ALWAYS ASK HER
IF SHE WANTS TO
COME OVER FOR
COFFEE.
MAKE SURE TO DO THIS
AFTER YOU HAVE LEFT
THE NOTE.

Use these letters for your note.

The next page has been left blank intentionally.

You will need a left-handed scissors and clear packaging tape.

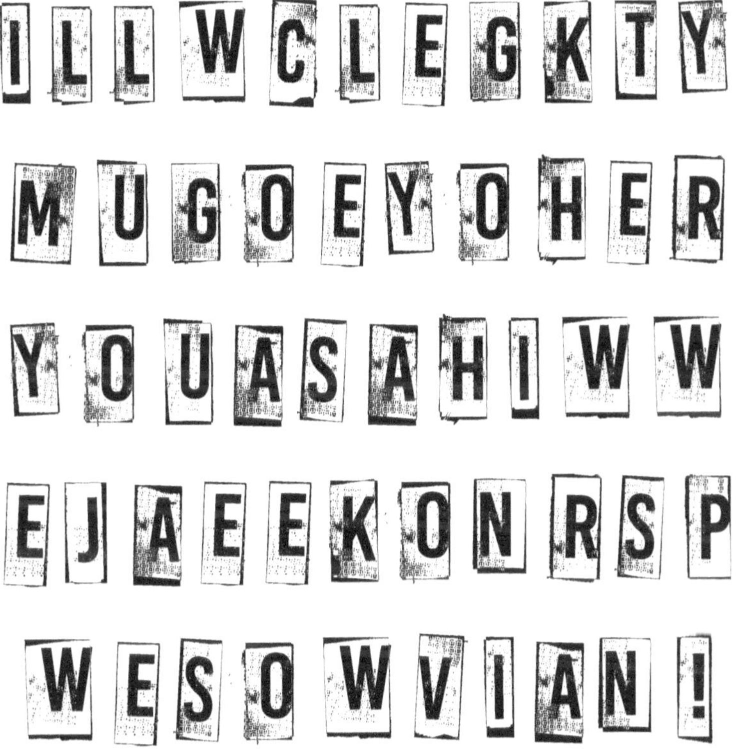

RUN!

WOMEN LOVE WHEN THEIR DATES LET THEM KNOW HOW THEY DID ON THEIR MAKEUP AND CLOTHING SELECTION. MAKE SURE YOU LET HER KNOW WHAT SHE NEEDS TO IMPROVE.

ALSO, ASK HER AGE
AND LET HER
KNOW IF YOU LIKE HER
BETTER WITH HER HAIR UP
OR DOWN.

MAKE SURE THAT HER
STYLE IS APPROPRIATE
FOR HER AGE.
LET HER KNOW IF YOU
FEEL IT ISN T.

Use this page to draw the clothing, hairstyle, and makeup you feel is appropriate for your date. Mail this to her before your next date.

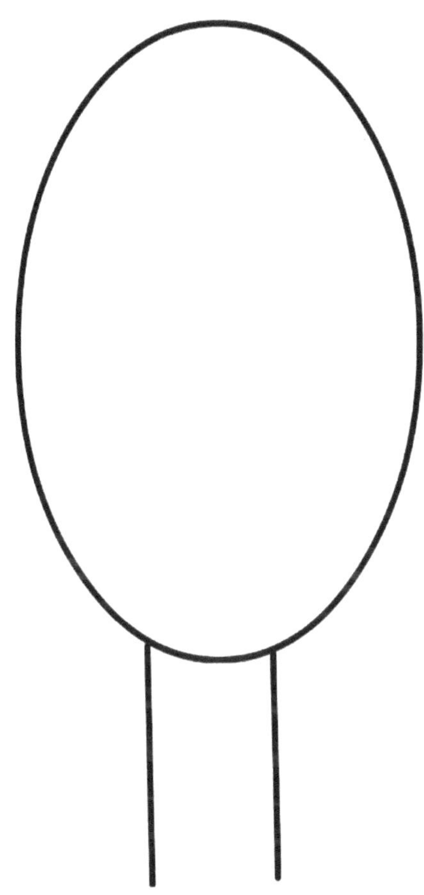

USE THE NEXT PAGES TO WRITE YOUR OWN TIPS SO YOU CAN REMEMBER THEM AND PASS THEM ON.

GOOD LUCK WITH YOUR DATE!

DISCLAIMER:

This book is designed to provide information to my readers. It is sold with the understanding that the publisher is not engaged to render any type of psychological, legal or any other kind of professional advice. No warranties or guarantees are expressed or implied for any content in this book. Neither the publisher nor the author shall be liable for any physical, psychological, emotional, financial, or commercial damages, including, but not limited to, special, incidental, consequential or other damages. You are responsible for your own choices, actions, and results.